After the Rain

After the Rain

WILLIE M. MEWBORN

authorHOUSE®

AuthorHouse™
1663 Liberty Drive
Bloomington, IN 47403
www.authorhouse.com
Phone: 1-800-839-8640

First published by AuthorHouse   10/17/2012

ISBN: 978-1-4670-2538-6 (sc)

Printed in the United States of America

Any people depicted in stock imagery provided by Thinkstock are models, and such images are being used for illustrative purposes only.
Certain stock imagery © Thinkstock.

This book is printed on acid-free paper.

> "And he shall be as the light of the morning,
> when the sun riseth, even a morning without
> clouds; as the tender grass springing out of the
> earth by clear shining after rain" (II Samuel 23:4)

Contents

Dedication

I dedicate "After The Rain" to Andre' Gorham. Unaware, Andre' was such an inspiration to me when I first began to write. Each of these poems were some of the first pieces of poetry that I wrote after I met Andre'. He seemed to love writing just as much as I did. He also appeared to be a better writer than I. He really inspired me to write as he began to read some of my work. I could not believe that he really liked it. Because of his response I felt more at ease with my work. Before, I was a bit timid and afraid to let anyone read anything that I had written because it was from my heart. I was afraid to open up my heart to anyone. Andre' really inspired me to continue writing and not become afraid of what I had written. Without his inspiration and without the power of God many of my poems may never had been written! Many of them were just my way of dealing with life's inconveniences and the disappointments of life.

I also dedicate "After the Rain" to my family and dearest friends who prayed for me and stood by me during some of the most difficult times of my life. Thank you for your loving support and prayers. I struggled to get this book in print. There were many obstacles in my way. Many of which included time to proof-read the manuscript, rewrite the manuscript, computer issues, and of course financial issues. "But thanks be to God which always causeth me to triumph in Christ..." (II Corinthians 2:14) I can truly say that the very hands of God was in it all. I am constantly reminded of the lyrics from a well-known song, "God Did It.

I wrote each of these poems by the power and inspiration of the Holy Spirit. Many probably would never had been written had I been more mature and had I known more about God, Jesus Christ and the Holy Spirit. Through each poem I describe how I felt at that time in my life. I describe the impact that Jesus had on my life and how He changed my life. I also talk about my own inner doubts and struggles to really and truly trust in the Almighty God.

Many of the poems have been revised due to the fact that I have come to know the living God in a more intimate way. I wrote many poems out of pain, out of disappointment, and out of discouragement. When I really came to know God there was no more real pain, no more real disappointment, and no more discouragement. I can truly say, *"thanks be to God which giveth me the victory through my Lord Jesus Christ." (I Corinthians 15:57)* Blessed be the Name of the Lord!

Willie M. Mewborn
Author/Poet

1.
God's
Divine Love

"Beloved, let us love one another, for love springs from God, and he who loves his fellow men is born of God and is coming to know and understand God and is coming to recognize and get a clearer under-standing of God. And he who does not love has not become acquainted with God. He does not know God and he never did know God. For God is love. In this was the love of God displayed where we are concerned; in that God sent His Son, the only begotten or unique Son, into this world so that we might live through Him." (1 John 4:7-9)

The love of God is the greatest love there is. There is no greater love. Nor can any one find any other love that they consider greater than the manifested loved of God. There is none. God's divine love for mankind is so great that He laid down His life for our sins through the form of His Son, Jesus the Christ, the anointed one. Jesus literally took our place and died in our stead. God is so holy that sin demanded a penalty and someone had to be sacrificed for that sin. But then His love was so great for mankind that He offered Jesus up to die in our place. There is no greater love than the love God displayed toward us through our Lord, Jesus Christ. John tells us that, "God so greatly loved and dearly prized the world that He gave up His begotten and unique Son, so that whoever believes in Him, trusts in Him and relies on Him may not perish or be lost, but have eternal and everlasting life." (John 3:16)

Who Is A Friend?

A friend is someone who
Knows all about me,
Yet cares for me still!

A friend is someone who
Cares in spite of all,
I may say or do!

A friend is someone who
Stands by my side,
Even when others walk away!

A friend is someone who,
Loves me in spite of myself,
And stands by my side at all times!

A friend is someone who,
Accepts me, loves me and cares for me,
And respects me in every way!

Only In Jesus

Jesus is my life!
He is my reason for being,
My reason for living,
Only in Him,
Can I truly live,
And be at rest!
I'm free to choose,
His way of life,
For He completes my life.
Because only in Him
Can I truly live, and move,
And have my being.
My longing to have Him near,
I can ne'er explain,
I can ne'er comprehend,
Because only He can,
Complete my life!

God . . .

Who is God?
No words can fully,
Describe the magnificent,
Content of His character.
Nor can words
Describe His Love,
His power,
His authority,
His majesty,
The awesome,
Power of His love,
In its' entirety!
For words can
Ne'er describe
This extraordinary
Being we call
GOD . . .
For His love for me
Transcends anything
This world has ever known!
For He is
God . . .
And God alone!

God Is . . .

God is . . . .
A wonderful God!
A magnificent God!
He loves beyond man's capacity,
To comprehend or understand!

God is . . .
A friend
Who's always near by,
He stands by my side,
When no one seems to care,
He lifts me high,
Up above all of my enemies!

God is . . .
A very good Friend
He looks beyond my faults,
He sees my heart!
He sees my need!

God is . . .
A Friend,
Who gives me hope,
When I've lost my way,
He takes my hand,
And leads me into His
Magnificent plans!

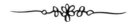

Thank You, Lord!

Thank You, Lord
for what you are to me!
You are my dearest Friend,
A Friend I can put my trust in!

Thank You, Lord
for all You've done for me!
You supply all of my need,
According to your riches in glory!

Thank You, Lord
for being my very best Friend,
You are my Lord, my God,
Who watches over me!

Thank You, Lord,
for walking with me,
during my time of need
When I need You most,
You're always at my side!

Thank You, Lord
for your Son, Jesus Christ
For He is the one
Who gave His all
To ransom me!
And I thank You, Lord!

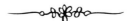

Jesus Christ Is . . . .

Jesus Christ is . . . .

The physician who . . .
Never lost a patient!

The attorney who . . .
Never lost a case!

The Judge who . . .
Dismisses all the charges

The jury who . . .
Pleads, "Not guilty!"

The friend who . .
Sticks closer than a brother!

The King who . .
Reigns forever and ever!

What Love!

Oh! what love God must possess,
To love me in spite of myself!

To walk with me,
When I turned back on Him!

To speak with me,
When I cared not to listen to Him!

To be my Friend,
When I saw no need for Him!

To shield me from danger,
When I felt no need for Him!

To die for me,
When I was lost in sin!

To stand by my side,
When I turned away from Him!

Oh! what love God must possess,
To love and care for me!

What Is Love?

What is love?
Can any words define it?
Can anyone explain it?
It is so mysterious,
That only God could design it!

Can anyone comprehend its depth?
Or its' vastness?
It's so wide that,
Only God can surround it!
It's so deep that,
Only He can reach its' peak!

This thing called "love",
Is so unique that,
It takes God to define it!
And so intriguing that
Only He could express it fully!

His Endless Love!

His Love is as endless,
and as infinite
as the ocean shore!

His Love has no bounds,
and no stipulations,
and has no limitations!

His Love reaches the highest mountains
and flows to the ends of the earth,
and through the lowest valleys!

His Love sweeps through our souls,
and reshapes our hearts,
as the refreshing ocean currents!

His Love soothes our burdened spirits,
and heals our troubled minds,
and calms all our lingering fears!

His Love is as endless as time,
and as deep,
as the Heavenly Shores!

His Love!

His love is by far
      The greatest love I've known!

No other love I know
      could sacrifice so much!
         and yet remain so strong!

No other love I know
      could reach the depths of hell
      and rise so victoriously!

No other love I know
      could love me so completely
      and yet be so unconditional!

No other love I know
      could commune with me
      and affect my life so amazingly!

His Love For Me!

Mere words can never describe,
His great Love for me!
There are not enough words,
In the world's vocabulary,
To describe the depth,
Of His Love for me!
No single word,
Could come close enough,
To express what I mean to Him!
For, I mean more,
Than words could ever express!
I mean more to Him,
Than anyone could ever know!
His Love for me,
Is greater than any,
Love I've ever experienced!
His love reaches,
To the highest mountain,
And the lowest valley,
With His love for me,
I simply rest in His divine presence,
And become complete, full and whole,
Because of His amazing Love for me!

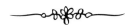

2.

My Love
For God

"You shall have no other gods before Me or besides Me."
(Deuteronomy 5:7) "And you shall love the Lord your God with
all your mind and with all your heart and with your entire being
and with all your might." (Deuteronomy 6:5)

The love of God for mankind is so great that it demands a change in our hearts, in our minds and in our characters. Once we come into fellowship with God through Jesus Christ our lives are changed forever. The greatness and power of His love demands a change in our lives. Because His love is so powerful and so awesome we have to respond to His love and to His power. Once we respond to Him our lives are changed forever. Our response comes in the form of our love for Him and our desire to worship and serve Him. What a great love God has that His love for us demands a response. Paul even encourages us that once we have this revelation that we are to "make a decisive dedication of your body and presenting all of your members as a living sacrifice, holy and devoted to God, which is your rational and intelligent service and spiritual worship." (Romans 12:1)

I Love You . . .

I love You because
You're so precious to me!

I love You because
You're so kind and understanding!

I love You because
You're so wonderful to me!

I love You because
You're so patient with me!

I love You because
Your Arms are always around me!

I love You because
You always hold my hand!

I love You because
You first loved me!

My Love For You

My love for You,
I may ne'er understand,
You mean more to me,
Than I could ever express!

I have no words,
To explain,
My love, my devotion,
My heartfelt gratitude!

Of all the things
I've come to know,
What more could I ask
But to live closer to You!

All I could ever dream,
Lies within my grasp,
As long as You're near,
I'm free to live!

And my love for you,
Will forever be,
A great mystery to me,
Always and forever!

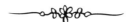

Like Jesus

I long to <u>be</u> like Jesus,
    This is my earnest plea,
His love within my life to show,
    That He lives within me!

I long to <u>live</u> like Jesus,
    His holy life through mine,
That all the world around may know,
    His life through me doth shine!

I long to <u>love</u> like Jesus,
    Indeed as well as word,
That everyone I see may know,
    That I glorify my Lord!

I long to <u>think</u> like Jesus,
    With holy thoughts and pure,
My mind consumed by His mind,
    In His great love secure!

I long to <u>see</u> like Jesus,
    Both eyes holy and pure,
My mind's eye clouded by His
    That I may become like Him!

My Friend, Jesus!
(PART I)

He is a Friend, like no other!
He is a Friend who is closer than any brother!

He walks with me each day of my life!
He walks with me dispelling all strife!

He speaks to me and calms all my fears!
He speaks to me and fills my heart with cheer!

He holds my hands throughout the day!
He holds my hands and teaches me how to pray!

My Friend, Jesus is a Friend indeed!
My Friend, Jesus is all I need!

He shields and protects with loving arms!
He shields and protects me from all harm!

He comforts me when I'm in need!
He comforts me indeed!

My Friend, Jesus!
(Part II)

Jesus is a Friend, like no other!
And is more precious to me,
       than the most precious jewels!

He speaks to me with great love,
And holds my hands
       and assures me that I am His own!

He walks close beside me!
And is my ever present Friend,
       who is with me always!

He understands my every thought!
And whispers peace to my soul,
       even when the storms continuously rage!

He cares for me like no other!
And supplies all my needs,
       in accordance to His mighty riches!

He is a Friend, like no other!
And is more precious to me,
       than all this world could ever offer!

I Love The Lord

I love the Lord,
Because He hears my cry!

I love the Lord,
Because He answers my prayer!

I love the Lord,
Because He first loved me!

I love the Lord,
Because He is so gracious!

I love the Lord,
Because He fills me with His Holy Spirit!

I love the Lord,
Because He holds my hands!

I love the Lord,
Because He speaks to my heart!

Because Of You!

Lord, in spite of all that happens,
About me and around me,
And in spite of all that I can see
I believe that every thing, will be all right!
Because You are at my side,
And with You in control of my life,
All things can't remain the same!
With You living within my heart and soul,
My life is full and complete!
With You touching my life,
I am truly blessed!
You take the confusion and strife I see,
And turn it into pure life!
I believe that everything will be all right,
And it's all because of You,
And your loving kindness towards me!

This Man

I fell-in-love one day,
With a man I love so dear,
With a man whose always near!

He has never forsakened me,
Nor has He ever left my side,
And He always supply all my need!

No other could love me so dearly!
No other could cherish me so!
No other could be so precious!

This Man I call, "Jesus"
Has changed my heart,
And has turned my life around!

This Man, I call "Jesus,"
Mere words could never describe,
The debt of love I owe to Him!

With Jesus

I long to be alone with Jesus,
    to really be alone with Him,
        because I cherish the moments.

I long to be in His presence
    to rest within His loving arms,
        and become complete.

I long for the moments,
    to sit at His feet,
        and feast upon His Words.

I long to hold His hands,
    to sit next to Him,
        and be at complete rest.

I long to be alone with Jesus!
    to conform into His Image,
        and become more like Him.

Jesus Cared For Me!

Jesus, I've come today to let You know,
That I love You more,
> than I could ever show!

You cared for me when others didn't!
You held my hands
> when others turned away!

You held me in Your Arms!
You walked beside me,
> when no one seemed to care!

Jesus, I love you more today!
And I love You most for
> laying down Your life for me!

Jesus Is Enough!
(PART I)

Jesus you are enough
to fill my soul!
and make me whole!

When I need You most
You answer my call
and you lift me when I fall!

When I'm weak,
You give me strength
and keep me from sins' brink!

When I'm lonely,
You walk with me
and set me free!

When fear grips my heart,
You hold my hand
for you are like no other man!

Jesus Is Enough!
(PART II)

Jesus is enough to walk with me,
    when I'm lonesome!

Jesus is enough to lift my spirit,
    when I'm sad!

Jesus is enough to fill my heart,
    when the billows roar!

Jesus is enough to dry my eyes,
    when the tears continue to flow!

Jesus is enough to wrap me in His Arms,
    when I need consolation!

Jesus is enough to supply all my needs,
    when other sources fail!

Jesus is more than enough
    to see me through every circumstance!

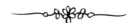

Why I Love You !

I love You, not so much
for what You can offer me,
or what you can give me!

Not just for the blessings,
that are stored up in Heaven,
and that You've given me!

Not just for holding my hand,
In my lowest moments
and when I needed it most!

Not just for wiping my face,
And drying my eyes,
when they filled with tears!

Not just for holding me
And shielding me from heartache,
When my heart was broken!

Not just for shielding me,
From dangers round about,
When the storm clouds rose!

Not just for giving me strength,
And making me strong,
when I cared not to go on!

Not just for walking with me,
And becoming my best Friend,
when others walked away!

Not just for whispering peace to me,
And dispelling all my fears,
when the billows roared!

But I love You most
for your loving support,
and Your great love for me!

And I love you still for being,
My ever-present God!

3.

Waiting On The Lord

"Have you not known? Have you not heard? The everlasting God, the Lord, the Creator of the ends of the earth, does not faint or grow weary; there is no searching of His understanding. He gives power to the faint and weary, and to him who has no might He increases strength and causes his strength to multiply. Even the youth shall faint and be weary and young men shall feebly stumble and fall exhausted; But those who wait for the Lord and hope in Him shall change and renew their strength and power; they shall lift their wings and mount up close to God as eagles mount up to the sun; they shall run and not be weary; they shall run and not faint or become tired." (Isaiah 40:28-31)

Throughout the scripture we are taught to wait on the Lord. From Genesis to Revelation there is an appeal to us to just wait on the Lord, trust in the Lord and to rest in His promises and to rest on His promises. This appeal may not always come easy to many of us. We may waver in our confidence in Him. One day we may trust Him and the next we may not have enough faith to even pray. Once we really come to know the Lord we can do as David the Psalmist encouraged us, "Wait and hope for the Lord, and expect the Lord; be brave and of good courage and let your heart be stout and enduring. Yes, wait for and hope for and expect the Lord." Whether we acknowledge it or not but waiting, depending, and trusting in the Lord is by far the greatest thing that any of us could ever do for ourselves. God is a sure foundation. He will never let us down. He will not bend or waver or even divert His ways from us. Throughout the scripture we are taught that we can depend upon Him and trust In Him. Solomon, the son of David encourages us to, "Lean on, trust in, and be confident in the Lord with all of your heart and mind and do not rely on your own insight or understanding. In all of your ways know, recognize, and acknowledge Him, and he will direct and make straight and plain your paths." (Proverbs 3:5-6)

Walk Beside Me!

Please walk beside me, dear Lord!
Hold my hands in the midst of trouble!
Plead my case precious, Lord!
Stand between me and all the trouble,
And any obstacles I may encounter!
When I begin to fall, dear Lord
Give me strength to stand tall!
Lord, prove to me that all power,
Is truly in your Holy and righteous hands!
Walk beside me, Lord,
Because only You can help me,
And give me the added strength,
Stamina and boldness,
To stand bold,
To stand strong,
 And become faithful!
Just walk beside me,
And guide me, dear Lord!

Teach Me How To Wait!

Lord, teach me how to become patient.
In all I say and do,
You see, it has not always been easy.
It's not something I was born with.
It's not something I learn with ease.

Some say that patience is a virtue.
Some say that patience comes from You,
Give me more of that "patient" power!
When I stand with my back to the wall,
Teach me to trust and depend upon You!

I have to wait and depend upon You,
For the things I desire in this life!
Teach me how to put my trust in You
Teach me how to wait on You, Lord
And depend upon your Holy Word!

Just teach me how to wait, Lord!
Teach me how to trust in You!
Teach me how to trust in your Word!
Teach me how to depend upon You!
Teach me to trust in You, my Lord!

Patience Is A Virtue . . .

I have been told that patience,
Is a virtue from God.
Can it be true,
That it's not always easy,
To wait as God asks,
Especially when I put my eyes,
On everything else but God?

Do I always wish to have things instantly,
And I feel that waiting,
And waiting on God is so tedious?
Do I feel that He is sometimes late,
And He may not answer on time?

How long does it take me to realize,
That God is just making and molding me,
After His image and likeness,
When he requires that I wait on Him!
And waiting on Him is really not bad!

Does things really fall apart,
When I have to wait on God?
Do I fail to see that in waiting on God,
I am being shaped and molded,
Into His own likeness and image?

Waiting On You

Lord, sometimes I felt that
    waiting on You was so obsolete,
      and a waste of my time.

I felt that You didn't understand,
    what I had to go through
      nor what I faced at all.

Sometimes I felt that You were a bit,
    slow in answering me,
      when I had to wait and wait!

Sometimes I felt that You might pass me by,
    and I would have no answer
      when I had to wait and wait!

Please teach me how to wait,
    and completely depend upon You,
      even when defeat stares right at me!

Why Do I Feel Discouraged?

Why do I feel discouraged when,
    I can't see the way?

Why do I feel discontented when,
    opportunities pass me by?

Why do I feel so lonely when,
    I have no one to confide in?

Why do I feel like giving up when,
    the whole world is against me?

Why do I feel hopeless when,
    all I have is a simple word?

Why do I have to see my way when,
    You promised to be my Guide?

Why do I feel discouraged when,
    You promised never to leave me alone?

You Promised!

Sometimes I felt that
everyday had to be bright,
and there was no reason for night!

I wished that You had promised,
that the sun would shine forever and ever,
and that there would be no rain!

I wished that You had promised,
that the world would always be pleasant,
and that there would be no more enemies!

I wished that You had promised,
that there would be no more trouble,
and that there would be no reason to cry!

But You did promise that,
You would give me peace,
that surpasses all understanding,
and that Your Son, Jesus would always
Light up my life!

A Brighter Day

In spite of all that happens, Lord,
I believe that everything,
Is going to be all right!

Sometimes I can look,
Through the pain,
And see a brighter day!

Sometimes, things get hard,
Down here Lord,
And I can't even see the Way!

I look at the sky,
And wish that I could,
See your precious Face!

I wish to hear your precious,
Still small voice,
When I pray, Lord!

Please hear my prayer Lord,
When I pray and keep me,
Looking for a brighter day!

When I Sit In Darkness
(Micah 7:8)

When I sit in darkness,
And dark clouds fill my life,
The Lord will be my Light!
When I fall, I shall arise,
Strength shall rise within my soul,
As I look upon His face!
I will wait upon the Lord,
And rest upon His promises
For He will answer me!
He will hear my cry,
He will plead my cause,
And bring me forth to the Light!
Shame shall cover mine enemies,
For they shall be trodden down!
God will lift me up,
For He is my stronghold,
When I sit in darkness!

Though The Storm Rages!

Though the storm begins to rage,
I'll keep my eyes upon that distant Shore!

Though darkness clouds out the sun,
I'll hold my head up high!

Though fierce winds begin to blow,
I'll find shelter in the arms of the Lord!

Though life may be drenched by the rains,
I'll keep my eyes upon my Home on high!

Though all my hopes lie scattered,
I'll find peace in the Word of God!

Though the storm continues to rage in my life,
I'll keep my hands in the hands of God!

I Will Wait Upon The Lord!
(Psalms 27)

I will wait upon the Lord,
and trust in His name
Because He will hear my cry!

I will wait upon the Lord,
And reach out to Him,
Because He will hold my hand!

I will wait upon the Lord,
and rest on His promises,
Because He will take care of me!

I will wait upon the Lord,
and call upon His name,
Because He will give me strength!

I will wait upon the Lord,
and pour out my soul to Him,
Because He will cleanse my heart!

I will wait upon the Lord,
and cast all my cares upon Him

Because He will answer my prayer!

4.
Soul
Searching

"Blessed be the Lord, because He has heard the voice of my supplications. The Lord is my strength and my impenetrable Shield; my heart trusts in, relies on and confidently leans on Him, and I am helped; therefore my heart greatly rejoices, and I praise Him. The Lord is my strength, and He is the stronghold of salvation to me His anointed." (Psalms 28:6-8)

Throughout our lives many of us have questions regarding who we are, what we are and what direction our lives should take. The same is true of God. We question who He is and what His role is in our lives. Many of us may even feel that we have no need for God or anything that He may have to offer us. We feel self-sufficient and have no need of God's services. Many of us fail to realize that it is through God that we learn who we are and what we are. We also find direction for our lives through Jesus Christ, our Lord. For it is through loving God, depending upon God, leaning upon God, and learning about God that we really learn who and what we are really all about. Jesus Christ is the sum total of what real life is all about. He is the life and He is our life. Many times Jesus spoke the words, "I am the way, the truth, and the life…"
(John 14:6)

No One But You!

Lord, sometimes I have,
No one to turn to,
No one to really trust,
No one, but You!

Sometimes, I have,
No one to talk to,
No one to really listen to me,
No one, but You!

Sometimes, I have,
No one to care for me
No one to really understand me,
No one, but You!

Sometimes, I have,
No one to lean on,
No one to really rely on,
No one, but You!

My Eyes On You

Lord, there are times no one seems to care!
No one seems to understand!
And I seem to travel this world all alone!
I feel that there is no one here,
No one here, but me!
I feel that there is no reason to go through,
No reason to really stand tall,
When I get my eyes off You!
There are times, Lord
Times I can look defeat in its face,
And smile with authority!
I feel there's a reason to go through,
I feel there is a reason to live,
There is a reason to go on,
And it seems that I'm not traveling alone,
I feel that there is someone at my side,
There is someone who really cares,
When I keep my eyes on You!

What Jesus Christ Has To Offer

Peace, He puts within my soul!

Joy, to carry me through each trial!

Patience,to endure hardships!

Temperance,to control my tongue!

Humility, just to teach me how to live!

Faith, to keep me within His care!

Hope, to keep me alive!

Love, to keep me at peace with others!

Gentleness, to keep me at peace with myself!

Victory, to proclaim that He is Lord of all!

Where Do I Go?

Where do I go,
When nothing seems to work,
When all falls apart,
And there is no where to turn,
And there's no hope for refuge?

Where do I go,
When my world seems to crumble,
And there's no one with hope,
And all seems dead,
All seems dead, but God?

Where do I go,
When life offers me sour lemons,
And I have no reason,
To hold on, no reason to go on?
Where do I turn, Lord?
 Where do I turn?

Do I turn to you, Lord,
And depend upon your Word?
Do I find real peace, real hope, real joy,
When I focus on You, Lord?
Do I find that peace, that joy,
That despells all fear?

Will You Help Me, Lord?

What can I say, Lord,
When there are many times,
When I feel so blue?
What can I say,
When I feel that things,
Are beyond my grasp?
I try to look up to the sky, Lord
And wonder how this,
Could be happening to me?
What can I say, Lord,
When I feel that all,
Has come to an end?
Will You open doors for me, Lord?
Will You open windows in Heaven?
Will You pour me out a blessing?
Will You give me that abundant life?
Will You give me that special hope?
Will You turn this around for my good?
Will you help me, Lord?

Where Do I Go From Here?

Where do I go from here, Lord,
When all has failed,
And everything has fallen apart,
And no one is standing by,
To lend me a helping hand?
Do I go on Lord,
And press my way through,
'Till I have a reason to go on,
Until I make it someday?
Can I hold onto your hand,Lord,
And hold on for dear life,
Until I cross that river,
Where I will find peace and happiness?
Where I'll find hope to go on,
Can I depend upon You, Lord
Until the end of time,
Can I depend upon You, Lord
To make my way plain,
Until I no longer have to ask,
"Where do I go from here?"

To Understand

Lord, help me to understand,
The reason for my cross,
 Help me to see your hand,
In all that happens to me,
That I my better follow You.
Help me to understand,
The reason for so many problems,
So many burdens,
That come my way.
Help me to understand,
That there is a price for,
Continual peace and tranquility,
And that through the storms,
I'm drawn closer and closer to You.
Help me to understand,
That I don't need a world of friends,
'To keep me company,
But that my life is full and complete,
With You at standing at my side.
Lord, help me to understand,
More and more about You,
Help me to see,
That all that happens to me,
Is shaped, molded and grafted,
Within your precious, holy hands!

5.
Trusting
In The Lord

"Who is among you who reverently fears the Lord, who obeys the voice of His servant yet who walks in darkness and deep trouble and has no shining splendor in his heart, Let him rely on, trust in and be confident in the name of the Lord, and let him lean upon and be supported by his God." (Isaiah 50:10)

Trusting in the Lord and in His Name is by far one of the greatest things any human being could do ever do for himself. At the time I was learning to trust in God I felt that it was a tedious chore that would only bring me heartache or shame. I knew so little of what faith in God can do. Learning about God and coming to know God comes through faith in Him. We can not please God except we have faith in Him. Paul even tells us that we learn to trust God by faith. "We walk by faith and regulate our lives and conduct ourselves by respecting our relationship to God and divine things, with trust and holy fervor, thus we walk not by sight or appearances." (11 Corinthians 5:7)

Teach Me To Trust In You

Lord, teach me to trust in You,
    And depend upon your faithfulness.

Teach me to believe in Your Holy Word,
    And lean upon your promises.

Teach me to live righteous and holy,
    And walk within your ways.

Teach me to hold onto your Hands,
    And rest in your everlasting Arms.

Teach me to give more of myself,
    And model my life after Jesus.

Teach me to walk with patience
    And be of good courage.

Teach me Lord, to trust in You,
    And wholly depend upon You!

Teach me to yield my entire life to You,
    And fully commit myself to You.

Jesus Opened Doors!

Jesus, you opened doors that I could not see.
You took my hand and walked beside me.
You made a way out of no way!

When I was at the end of the road,
You stood beside me,
And there was your hand for me to hold!

When I was at the end of my rope,
You held onto my hand,
And You gave me strength to hold on!

When I lost all hope,
You put a smile within my heart,
And gave me strength to stand!

When You continued to hold my hand,
You transformed my life,
And gave my life new meaning!

Thanks Lord!

Thanks Lord, for being so good!
You stood by my side when others walked away!

Thanks Lord, for what You are to me!
You are more than enough to meet my needs!

Thanks Lord, for all You've done for me!
You have done marvelous things!

Thanks Lord, for being my best Friend!
You are the greatest Friend I've ever known!

Thanks Lord, for the peace You put within my soul!
You are my peace and the strength of my life!

Thanks Lord, for caring when no one else cared!
You laid down your life for me!

Thanks Lord, for Your precious Son, Jesus!
You gave Him that I might live abundantly!

I Will Praise You Lord!

I will praise You, Lord even though the storm rages,
  And the billows continue to roar!

I will praise You, Lord though the way grows dark,
  And the road seems all uphill!

I will praise You, Lord though the thunder continues to roar,
  And the lightning continues to flash!

I will praise You, Lord though my days are dreary,
  And storm clouds continue to cover the sky!
'
I will praise You, Lord though darkness fills the sky,
  And the rain drenches out the sun!

I will praise You, Lord though I walk on sinking sand!
  And the valley sinks deeper each day!

I will praise You, Lord though I seem to walk alone,
  Because I know You walk with me!

I Will Stand!

I will stand and trust in the Lord,
no matter what the outcome!

I will stand and trust in the Lord,
though the fierce winds blow!

I will stand and trust in the Lord,
though floods try to drown out my life!

I will stand and trust in the Lord,
though the path seems all uphill!

I will stand and trust in the Lord,
though life throws out sour lemons!

I will stand and trust in the Lord,
though the lightning continues to flash!

I will stand and trust in the Lord,
though the thunder continues to roar!

I will stand and trust in the Lord,
because the Master holds my hands!

Unto The Hills!
(Psalms 121)

When cares press me down,
and my heart is grieved,
I will lift mine eyes,
unto the hills!

When friends cease to understand,
and I need a helping hand,
I will lift mine eyes,
unto the hills!

When debts are high,
and funds are low,
I will lift mine eyes,
unto the hills!

When my way seems dark,
and I've lost my direction,
I will lift mine eyes,
unto the hills!

When I despair of life,
and the nights are long and cold
I will lift mine eyes,
unto the hills!

When I feel discouraged,
and I have no strength to go on.
I will lift mine eyes,
unto the hills!

When I call upon the Lord
and He answers me,
I will lift mine eyes,
unto the hills from,
whence cometh all of my help!

Press On Still!

When trials come on every hand,
  I will press on still!

When darkness clouds my days,
  I will press on still!

When burdens press me down,
  I will press on still!

When I've lost my direction,
  I will press on still!

When all my dreams lie shattered,
  I will press on still!

When all my efforts seem all in vain,
  I will press on still!

When all hope seems lost,
  I will press on still!

When I hold onto His Hands,
  surely,I will press on!

Your Still, Small Voice

Don't ever stop smiling on me,
For I'll grow lonesome!

Don't ever stop shielding me,
For I'll be wounded!

Don't ever let go of my hands,
For I'll slip in the sinking sand!

Don't ever stop leading me
For I'll be lost!

Don't ever stop looking upon me,
For I'll miss your presence!

Don't ever take your joy from me,
For I'll grow weary!

Don't ever stop speaking to me,
For I'll miss your still,
small voice!

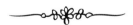

6

Victorious
Through Jesus Christ!

"But thanks be to God , Who gives us the victory and making us conquerors through our Lord, Jesus Christ." (I Corinthians 15:57) "But thanks be to God, Who in Christ always lead us in triumph as trophies of Christ's victory and through us spreads and makes evident the fragrance of the knowledge of God everywhere." (II Corinthians 2:14)

Those of us who live in the likeness of our Lord, Jesus Christ are walking in victory. We have victory over our circumstances, victory over sin, victory over Satan, and victory in every area of our lives. It is our God given right to walk in victory simply because God is standing at our side walking with us every step of the way. He even sends His ministering angels to watch over us each day of our lives. They are available to help us at any given moment. We do not have to lead a defeated life. We do not have to keep our eyes upon our circumstances and the situations that are surrounding us. The angels are always at our side to lift us up lest we dash out foot against a stone. David the Psalmist encourages us, "There shall no evil befall you, nor any plague or calamity come near your tent. For He will give His angels special charge over you to accompany and defend and preserve you in all your ways of obedience and service. They shall bear you up in their hands, lest you dash your foot against a stone. You shall tread upon the lion and the adder, the young lion and the serpent shall you trample under foot. Because he has set his love upon me, therefore will I deliver him; I will set him on high, because he knows and understands my name.." (Psalms 91: 10-14)

A Clean Heart!

Create within me a pure and clean heart!

Renew within me a righteous and holy spirit!

Despell all doubt and make me whole again!

Give me strength to hold onto your hands!

Help me relinquish my heart and soul to you!

Empty all slothfulness from my heart!

Give me feet like hind's feet!

Help me to acknowledge you in all my ways!

Create within me a clean heart, dear Lord!

And renew within me the right spirit!

Next To Me

God sat beside me today!
He held my hand!
And Oh! the joy,
That flooded my soul,
When He sat next to me!

My heart was overwhelmed,
As we walked hand in hand!
The world was magnificent,
Beyond compare,
When God walked beside me!

As I beheld His face,
His eyes shone brilliantly,
That I was almost blinded,
But, Oh! the peace,
That filled my heart,
When I looked upon His face!

When He spoke to me,
The world stood still!
He assured me of His endless love,
Of His abiding presence,
And what blessed quietness filled my soul,
When God spoke peace to my heart!

Prisoner!

I went to prison one day!
I was pushed behind bars!
Everything was dark and gloomy!
As I looked around for Jesus!
He was nowhere in sight!

Chains seemed to strangle me!
Shackles paralyzed my legs!
I couldn't move freely!
I was bound completely!
What was I to do?

I didn't need the Lord!
Or did I?
Did I need anything He had to offer?
Did I need His plans for my life?
His way was so obscure!

One day I grew tired!
Tired of chains! Tired of shackles!
Tired of restraints! Tired of roadblocks!
Where was the freedom that He offered!

I looked to Him! He gave me freedom!
He broke the chains! He broke the shackles!
The chains are broken since He set me free!
And no longer am I a prisoner to this world!

He Opened My Eyes!

When He lifted the veil from my eyes,
 My life took on new meaning!

Problems disappeared in His presence
As we walked hand in hand!

I watched my cares melt at His feet
As He began to speak to me!

Difficulties were His opportunities,
To perform miracles in my life!

Cares were instruments He used,
To keep me within His will!

Problems were the puzzled-fragments
That He used to shape me into His likeness!

Obstacles were the tools,
To keep my eyes upon Him!

My eyes are open now
That I see Him in the midst of the storms!

To Know Him!

I long to know Him!
To really get to know Him!
In His power, might and majesty!

To witness His power,
And get to know Him,
Until my faith is limitless!

To walk in His majesty
Until He reigns as King,
Upon the throne of my life!

To live within His greatness,
Until He is Lord of all,
The kingdoms of my heart!

I long to walk in His footsteps,
And experience His compassion,
Until my steps are Heavenward!

I Am Persuaded!
(Romans 8:38)

When trouble comes
    and I feel faint,
        I am persuaded!

When friends turn away,
    and I feel lonesome,
        I am persuaded!

When bills accumulate,
    and I have no funds,
        I am persuaded!

When loved ones pass,
    and I bow in sorrow,
        I am persuaded!

When defeat seems eminent,
    and I fell like giving up,
        I am persuaded!

When all efforts seem in vane,
    and all seems lost,
        still, I am persuaded!

They Say . . . .

They say You rule the mighty universe!
Oh! what power You must possess,
To rule such a vast domain!

They say You calmed the raging sea!
You divided that great river!
You stopped the rain for three years!

They say You opened deaf ears!
You caused the lame to walk again!
You opened the blinded eyes!

They say You can do anything!
You healed the broken-hearted!
You transformed the sinner's hearts!

They say You set the captives free!
You broke the bonds of prison!
You gave your life for an old sinful world!

Stranger!

I wonder what you would do,
If a stranger visited you?
Not knowing that it was Jesus,
Would you welcome Him into your home,
As an honored guest?
Would you trust Him enough,
To allow Him to stay over night,
And take a while to rest?
Would you allow Him,
To stay a day or two
And make Himself at home?
Would you allow Him to give you
All the things you needed,
Much needed wisdom, knowledge and advice?
I wonder what you would do if,
Jesus stood knocking at your heart's door,
And asked to make Himself at home?

In Search Of My God!

I wandered out one day,
Alongside the street,
In search of my God!
As I felt a tug at my heart,
I looked toward Heaven,
And felt closer to my God!
For, I was on a journey,
In search of my God!
As I felt another tug at my heart!
I fell to my knees,
And emptied my heart!
He filled me with His Love!
Joy and happiness far untold,
Filled my soul!
I found everything I needed,
And more,
When I wandered down the streets,
In search of my God!

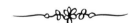

I'm Blessed . . . .

I'm blessed Lord,
Thanks to You!

You cared for me,
   And stood by my side
Even when others could care less!

You opened doors,
   And kept them open
When they were slammed in my face!

You picked up the pieces of my life
   And rearranged them,
Even when they were scattered among the leaves!

You lifted the burdens,
   And gave me strength
When my heart continued to ache!

You found me,
   And filled my soul with your peace,
When I was lost along life's highway!

Truly, I'm blessed, Lord
Because of You,
And your great love for me!

Impossible?

Incorrigible? Impossible?
No! Not at all!
No! Not with God!

Some things impossible!
Some people incorrigible!
Paths you can't cross!

Mountains you can't tunnel through?
God specializes in impossibility!
He can do anything!

Got friends you thing are incorrigible?
Try God! He proves otherwise!
Anything too hard for Him?

Paths uncrossable?
Mountains intangible?
People incorrigible?

No! Not at all!
No! Not with God!
Impossible situations? Try God!

The Pathway To Happiness

I found the path to happiness!
I desired the company of my friends!
Surely, they could enhance my joy!
I looked everywhere as I walked!
There were so many opportunities!
I wondered which to choose!
I was filled with so much joy!
What consolation to have friends along!
We shared everything in life!
Many Months passed by!
Slowly, my friends drifted away!
"Will they turn back on me?" I thought.
Suddenly they turned away from me!
My world was shattered!
"How could they leave me all alone?" I cried!
"Happiness is to be shared," I reasoned.
Life is lonely with no one to share!
Life is meaningless!
"What will I do?"

I felt so empty as I stood silent,
I took a long look down that path!
On one side I saw Jesus!
"Was He there to walk with me?" I thought.
Could He give me the joy I longed for!
Did I really need Him?
Could He complete my life?
I walked over to Him!
Could He give me everything I needed?
Would He hold my hand?
Would He direct my path?
Could He do that for me?
He took my hand!
He stole my heart!
He pulled me into His arms,
As we began walking down the rugged path,
He led me up the rocky road!
He gave me peace far untold!
When He walked with me,
On the pathway to happiness!

7.
God's
Redeeming Love . . .

"For God so greatly loved and dearly prized the world that He even gave up His only begotten Son, so that whoever believes in, trusts in, clings to and relies upon Him may not perish, but have eternal and everlasting life. For God did not send the Son into the world in order to judge, reject, condemn or pass sentence on the world, but that the world might find salvation and be made safe and sound through Him."

(John 3:16, 17) "But this is the bread that comes down from Heaven, so that anyone may eat of it and never die. I am this living Bread that came down from Heaven. If anyone eats of this Bread, he will live forever, and also the Bread that I shall give for the life of the world is my flesh, my body." (John 6: 50, 51)

God's love for man was so great that He could not stand by and watch man live and die in sin. Mankind was so wrapped up into sin. Because God is so holy, He could not allow man to stand before Him tangled up into sin. Because of His great love for mankind, He sent His Son Jesus to die in man's stead. Sin demanded a penalty and Jesus paid that penalty by laying down His life. That was the greatest expression of God's love for man when Jesus sacrificed His life for the life of mankind. Man's sin had separated him and God. Fellowship was broken. To restore that relationship Jesus gave His life. The power of sin was broken and fellowship between man and God was restored. That redemption or restoration demanded the shedding of blood. Jesus Christ was the only one worthy to stand before God on man's behalf. He laid down His life on man's behalf that man may be able to stand before God holy and righteous. The living Bread from Heaven, literally came down to earth to offer to mankind a brand new, wholesome life.

Jesus Walked With Me!

Jesus walked with me,
When my way was so obscure!
When my past was so bleak!
My present was so uncertain!
There were habits I could not break!
There were mountains I'd dare not climb!
Dreams that never reached the sky!
Yet, I had no faith in God!
Could He change my life?
Could He make a difference in my life?
But how could I allow Him to?
Could He erase the pain?
Could He erase the past?
One day He walked with me!
In a moment's time, He erased my past!
He put the light of his life into my heart!
He gave me hope like no other!
My dreams now reach to His heart!
I can see the invisible!
I can feel the intangible!
I can rest within His Word!
My faith looks Heavenward,
Since Jesus walks with me!

Looking Back!

I have heard the saying,
"One should never look back into the past!"
"Let by-gones be by-gones."
"You can't change the past."
But when I look back over my life,
My heart is overwhelmed,
By the power of God's hand in my life!
My eyes fill with tears of joy,
Just recalling how He walked with me,
When darkness clouded my life!
There were times I felt hopeless!
I had sank to rise no more!
But His grace and mercy brought me through!
My path was rough and rugged!
My body was tired from life's journey!
But He always gave me strength to go on!
So, when I look back over my life,
My heart is filled with worship and gratitude,
Of how He held my hands,
And carried me along the way!

Promised Land!

I've glimpsed the promised land!
I dare not travel alone!
The land where few tread,
Who will share it with me?
Will I travel alone?
Alone . . . . alone . . . . No! Not alone!
Mountains to climb?
Because I have overcome!
Rugged pathways to cross?
But, Oh! Not alone!
Road blocks to pass?
Oh! what high achiever I am
Valleys to tredge through?
I dare not stop!
Obstacles to overcome,
Just to reach the top,
As I travel this pathway of life!
Dreaming the impossible!
Running this race patiently with Jesus!
Reaching for the sky!
My goal is Heaven!
My limits are found within Jesus,
Because I've glimpsed
The promised land!

Highway To Heaven

As I started out on this road,
There were many obstacles in my way,
I crossed many puddles,
That appeared to be rivers!
There were many mountains I had to climb,
They merely became hills!
And the valleys that I encountered,
Became my resting place!
Road blocks that stopped me in my tracks,
Became the training ground for success!
Hopeless situations that broke my heart,
Became the stepping stone to greatness!
Friends who turned their backs on me,
Were instruments to refine my faith in God
Little funds, low funds and no funds,
Were reassurances of God's provision!
Because I've had a glimpse,
Of the highway that leads,
Straight to my heavenly home!

He Reigns!

When trouble comes,
And defeat seems pre-eminent,
Satan seems to triumph victoriously!
But God reminds me,
"I'm just making and molding you!" (Jere. 18:6)

When all I've accomplished,
Has fallen into a million pieces,
Satan stands and snickers relentlessly!
But I must always remember,
"God's ways are higher than our ways!" (Isa.55:9)

When loved ones have gone on,
And I bow in loneliness and sorrow,
Satan sends dark clouds of gloom,
God assures me again and again,
"The dead in Christ shall rise again!" (Rom. 4:17)

When storm clouds rise,
And all is bleak,
Satan brings fear, gloom and defeat!
But God proclaims to me,
"My grace is sufficient for you!" (11Corin. 12:9)

When friends turn back on me,
Satan laughs bringing loneliness and rejection!
In the foreground my God shouts,
"I'll never leave you nor forsake you!"(Joshua 1:5)

When my way seems dark and dreary,
Satan whispers hopelessness and failure!
But I can hear Jesus shouting,
"I am the way, the truth and the life!" (John 14:6)

When miracles seem to be a thing of the past,
Satan lies and whispers,
"God has forgotten you! There are no miracles!"
I am reminded of God's Word,
"All things work together for good to those
who love God." (Romans 8:28)

8.

Conclusion

"Oh that my words were now written, Oh that they were printed in a book! That they were inscribed with an iron tool on lead, or engraved in a rock forever! I know that my Redeemer lives and that in the end he will stand upon the earth." (Job 19:23-25)

Job had suffered so much pain and disappointment during his life. He lost his children, his home and even lost his health. He could not understand why God would allow him to go through so much suffering and pain. He even tried talking to his friends to gain a better understanding of why bad and tragic things happened to him. His friends were so hurt and despondent that even they could not explain why Job was under so much attack. They tried to comfort Job but didn't know how. In the end Job began talking to God and questioning God as why the tragic events came into his life. God answered Job and eventually restored to Job all the valuable things he had lost.

I can sympathize with Job but I have no way of understanding the depth of Job's pain and loss. But I can sympathize with Job's desire to write, to tell his story, to get it out in order to relieve some of the pain he was feeling. He wanted to pour out his soul in order to gain some healing, some relief from pain and heartache. Getting things out of one's system has a way of helping to heal the person. It seems to make dealing with the pain and heart-ache a bit easier to bear. At this point I can truly say that I write in order to deal with whatever I am facing. When it seems that I have no one to talk to I turn to writing in order to cope and deal with life's frustrations. It seems to give me some added strength when I put into writing what I am feeling or what I'm faced with. I can say with Job, "oh, that my words were written and printed in a book." (Job 19:23)

When rain comes into our lives, it comes in several different ways. It can come as a sprinkle, as a drop, as a drizzle, as a continuous slow rain or as a continuous down pour. The rain can last for one second, one minute or one hour or maybe even longer. Along with all the rain, storm clouds can rise and the winds will begin to blow. The clouds may or may not grow darker and that darkness can also be measured in different hues and shades. But regardless of the different levels and degrees and directions, rain is rain, and it comes into each of our lives. Many of us may see the rain as a detriment to our lives and there are others who may see the rain a necessity to make our lives fruitful. And our response to the storm and the rain determines how it will affect our lives.

I titled my first book, "Through the Storms and Through the Rain." I wrote many poems about the difficulties in my life and how I dealt with each of them. I learned many things while writing my first book. Facing difficulties came very hard for me because I felt that I was dealing with them alone. The difficulties created so much unrest and uneasiness. Many times I felt that God was punishing me for some wrong that I had committed. I felt that God had walked away from me and that He had no idea how bad I was feeling. I yearned to be free of difficulties, heart-ache, disappointment and pain. I often wondered where was God in the midst of all this heart-ache.

As I was finishing my first book, I began hearing God speak to me. As I began writing, He began speaking. He began to teach me many lessons and I often write about them through my poems. Even though I was hurting, I was not alone. Even though I felt that I was dying, I was very much alive. Even though I felt that God was a million miles away, He was always at my side. Even though I felt so alone and so unloved, I learned that God is always with me and He will never leave me standing alone. Many times throughout my life I hated the rain that came into my life. I hated the storms and I was often afraid of the thunder storms and the lightning that often accompanied them. I hated them all and often wondered why God allowed such things.

God showed me that the rain was very much needed in our lives. God showed me that there is beauty, freshness and growth after the rain. Though it seems that we don't need the rain at times, God understands the reasons behind the down pours, the wind, the thunder and the lightning that often accompanies it. After the rain, flowers bloom, the earth is replenished with much needed water, plants grow, grass and other vegetation grows, the food we eat grows. God assured me that rain did not have to represent dark clouds, gloom or doom. It did not have to represent disappointment and pain.

There is a refreshing aroma after the rain. That is one of the things God wanted me to focus my attention on. The refreshing aroma, the cleansing aroma, the scent of newness, the scent of a new life is what God wanted me to focus my attention on. God is full of life and surely I could see life when I turned my eyes on Him.

While I was writing, "After the Rain," I still had questions concerning the loud thunder that sometimes accompanies the rain. I still had questions concerning the lightning that flashed and the dark clouds that sometimes seem to hang low. But through these questions God taught me that I don't have to be afraid of the storms. I don't have to hide from the dark clouds or the loud thunder. I don't have to hide from the rain. I can enjoy its' freshness and its' aroma as it falls to the earth. I don't have to be afraid because He is in control of it all. Nothing catches Him off guard. He knows all about the storm and the rain and the dark clouds. He is the all powerful God who sees all, knows all and is control of all things.

After I began to learn more about the part God plays in the storm and the rain, I began to understand more about the fragrance after the rain. It is that fragrance, that aroma, that I focus the majority of my poems. I have learned that rain will come into our lives but it doesn't have to destroy us when it comes. It doesn't have to consume us. Even a wind and rain storm has a creative purpose. If only I look for the purpose that God put in it instead of dreading the storm when it arrives then I can see the beauty of it all. Fresh, new life will surely come after the rain if I will but focus on the purpose of the almighty God. I will conclude with one of the most insightful poems that I have ever written.

When I Thought . . . .

When I thought that I would die,
It was then that God was taking out of my life,
All the things that would kill me!

When I thought that my life had no meaning,
It was then that God was reshaping my life,
To give me life to the fullest extent!

When I thought that God was angry with me,
It was then that He was revealing to me,
The things that were not pleasing to Him!

When I thought that God was punishing me,
It was then that He was whispering peace to my heart,
And preparing my life for a blessing!

When I thought that God did not love me,
It was then that He was cleansing my heart and soul,
And preparing my life for greatness!

When I thought that God had let me down,
It was then that He was shielding me in His arms,
And whispering peace to my soul!

When I thought that God had forgotten about me,
It was then that He was reshaping my life,
And skillfully placing me within His divine will!

When I thought that God had turned His back on me,
It was then that He was making and molding me,
And shaping my character after His own!

When I thought that the tears would never cease,
It was then that God was breaking my will,
Until my life was shaped after His life!